MW01505595

POETRY BY CHANCE

AN ANTHOLOGY OF POEMS
POWERED BY METAPHOR DICE

Edited by

Taylor Mali

Button Publishing Inc.

Minneapolis

2023

POETRY BY CHANCE
AN ANTHOLOGY OF POEMS POWERED BY METAPHOR DICE
POETRY
EDITED BY: Taylor Mali
COVER DESIGN: Amy Law
COVER ART: Emily Van Cook
INTERIOR PHOTOGRAPHY: Peter Dressel

Published by Button Poetry
Minneapolis, MN 55418 | http://www.buttonpoetry.com

Manufactured in the United States of America
PRINT ISBN: 978-1-63834-074-4
EBOOK ISBN: 978-1-63834-075-1
AUDIOBOOK ISBN: 978-1-63834-076-8

First printing

POETRY BY CHANCE

AN ANTHOLOGY OF POEMS
POWERED BY METAPHOR DICE

FOREWORD

Every human culture that has ever lived has invented some form of metaphorical expression to help us talk about the *big things* in our lives that might otherwise be hard to understand. Difficult concepts and complex ideas like love, death, home, our relationships to one another—even our own identities—are often better communicated if we equate them to smaller objects that are simpler or just more familiar. That's what metaphors are for. Which is to say, any time a person begins a sentence with "Think of it this way . . ." they're probably about to use a metaphor, whether they realize it or not.

The idea for Metaphor Dice came to me after I told a self-professed math/science student that a metaphor is really just *an equation between an idea and a thing*. That was enough to pique her interest, but it took me another 15 minutes to explain the difference between abstract nouns and concrete nouns. I realized then that figurative language should be taught backwards. Instead of explaining what metaphors are first and then demanding a few creative examples as proof of understanding, switch that order around. First offer up a thousand random examples of metaphors—some good, some hysterically bad, and maybe others that are surprisingly enlightening—until you stumble on one that feels like it's begging you to explore how it's true and shows up in your experience.

Metaphor Dice can provide a starting place for a poem, but they can't write the next lines for you, the lines that will artfully demonstrate *why* the metaphor is apt and useful. That's the hard part, but it's often where the real poetry is found. As a result, ever since Metaphor Dice first appeared in 2018, people have been asking—especially teachers—for a collection of finished poems that others have written with the help of the dice. What you hold in your hands now is the first collection of such examples, including the two winners of The Golden Die Contest.

Every poem in this book is paired with an image of the exact roll of the dice that prompted the metaphor it uses. The dice in these images will always be in the same order—Concept, Adjective, Object—regardless of how the actual metaphor might have been ordered and crafted. Furthermore, the red, white, and blue dice—or as reproduced to black, white, and grey—will often be given their own page. We hope this makes it easier to include, exclude, or highlight the roll itself when considering these poems. And of course, you should feel free to fill all that blank space with your own notes, questions, and poems.

The winning poems from the adult and student contests appear first. After that it will not take long to figure out exactly how the rest of the poems in this anthology have been ordered.

—*Taylor Mali*

CONTENTS

POETRY BY CHANCE

AN ANTHOLOGY OF POEMS
POWERED BY METAPHOR DICE

UKRAINE

below
in the shelter
crouched together
holding hands

we light candles
   we pray
      we wait

the light

flutters
  dips
    bounces

hope is a silent dance

—Sandra Vaisnoras

NOT LIKE HOME

Isolation is a smalltown mirror.
On the Highstreet of Sheringham
I can't see my reflection.

The seagulls order fish & chips
and flock to the beach where I feel
their stares like lashes on my back.

I want to have fun like my sister
who blends into the crowd,
but I am the color of wet sand

and stand out like the rusty pillars
holding the white platform
for their enjoyment.

—Keiana Wolfe, age 10

LOSS,

　　　　that everyday animal, dogs me.
Panting, it crowds my knees
as I head to the kitchen for coffee,
nips at my heels as I climb the stairs
to dress, sticks its nose in my crotch
while I pull on my coat. I thought

I was a cat person, that Loss kept
its distance, showed up mostly at
feeding time, didn't care much
for attention. Days could go by
without Loss on my lap, kneading
my shoulder, curled beside me in

bed. But here it is again, claws
clattering, leash in its mouth, Loss
whining at the door, cocking its head,
its liquid eyes demanding to be taken
out for a walk. Every damn day.

　　　　　　　—Heidi Mordhorst

WHAT IT MEANS TO FORGET

For some,
forgetting is a gentle blessing
providing absolution
and forgiveness of sins.

For me,
forgetting is a harbinger of death,
bearing the image of my grandmother—
her brown eyes blank, blinking—
unable to remember my name.

—Carmela Martino

MY FATHER IS A SILENT BLESSING

My father is a silent blessing.
A lily in oak's bark.
For all his strength, conversation
is the only thing he can't seem to carry.

In his home, you had to learn
I love you was a tank of gas,
a copy of the new *Harry Potter*
brought home in his UAW lunchbox.

Now—years later—it is poorly timed,
jaw-loosening phone calls and iPhone pictures
of baby chicks and spotted calves.
Just born yesterday. Be sure to show Haley.

I love you too, Dad.

—*Matthew Hutchins*

I AM HEADING NORTH TO FORGET YOU

under the frostbitten sky and the
watchful shadows of skeleton pine trees,
I will exhale you like smoke.
But memory is a broken compass
and suddenly I am in Southern California
with the echo of your kiss on my salt lips.

—*Emily Sun Li*

BEAUTY IS A BURNING CURSE

Beauty is a burning curse.
The stares seem to attack
my skin and remind me
I can never be alone.

—*Josie, age 12*

DEATH IS A BURNING CURSE

I touch my mom's stomach
You aren't there anymore, you already left.

Screaming and running around the barren hospital room while
You lie there, chained in cords,
Beaten by the doctor and nurses that swarm you.

The next day is your funeral

A candle's light flickers across your casket;
A symbol of *should have been*
Your death is a burning curse

The older sister I was supposed to be
Holds memories of your tenth birthday
Your kindergarten graduation
Your running into her arms after school

—Things that never existed.

Your passing has left me frozen
A knife handed to me, covered in blood
Cutting my soul and reminding me of your flame

I blow out the candle
Holding the ashes in your pendant

Made with memories of you
Lying in that incubator
Chained in cords
Not even a whimper

While this big sister holds you in her arms
Squeezes you tight

And then you're gone.

—*Megan Forro, age 17*

PRINCE

After Ben Lerner

The past is an everyday curse.

I used to think that losers
only conjugate
            past tense verbs.
I was in the cage of a Ferris wheel,
and Lake Michigan felt close and far,
clouds clustered in the purple sky before it rained.
That day, I wanted to walk into the sea.

Ever since, the verbs started moving,
quick and blurry like stars.
Now the past is like a curtain.

I did not expect it,
but spring came in February,
alive as a deer.

Looking in the window,
the past is running away like a verb.
I will be adjusted for inflation.

I still get lost in the library.
Remember *The Little Prince*?
Tomorrow I will fly a spaceship full of cash,
and buy all the stars from a businessman.

                    —*Michael Liu, age 15*

TIME IS A BURNING CURSE

A curse of the body, a curse of the mind,
the flames of the fire, our lives on the line.
It heals all wounds but in the end takes us all,
the subtle ticking of the rise and the fall.

Our lives tick away as we watch, forlorn,
but we start to die from the moment we're born.
Impassable, strong, unfeeling and staid,
watching the world as we cower, afraid.

The burning inferno still stealing our years
until we are incapable of facing our fears.
The agony ripping open our wounds, the ticking,
      a stab in our heart,
the feeling of time passing: a burning, cursed art.

Until in the rubble surrounding us
there is nothing left but ash and dust.
But time is ever steady, ever strong.
It will be with us forever, all our life long.

The most complex object in the universe:
Is that the blessing of a curse?

—*Claire Furlanetto, age 12*

MEMORY CAUSES A SPECTACLE

Forgetting shines across the stage
He flexes his brown, blistered feet
As his dimples appear
His black eyes shut
                         His mind flies from his body
His head freezes
Pirouette, pirouette
            Arms lift and fall
Memory crumbles underneath his feet
            The orchestra in his brain falls flat
The wooden stage creaks
Ringing in his ears mutes the whispers from the seats
            Arms lift and fall
Dark white light dims his world
Arms lift
Memory flees
Forgetting stays
Forgetting is a rugged dance
He reaches for his mind
                  Reaches for his mind from across the theatre
Drags his arms across his body and leaps
Forgetting is a rugged dance
                                    Never finished

—Soa Andriamananjara, age 15

HOME IS AN ELUSIVE DANCE

home is an elusive dance
i spin an awkward tango with feeling out of place.
my motherland no longer feels like home,
neither does where i live.

i prance a clumsy foxtrot
getting seemingly farther from my language.
words trip and stumble in my mouth
and pile up in the back of my throat.

i sway a sad and bitter waltz
confronting my relationship with my birthplace.
it is become uncomfortable
a pair of too-tight shoes that i
continue to wear

i am (maybe just to myself)
always a foreigner.
but i can dance in outgrown shoes.
right?

—*Liv Trottier-Mitcheson, age 16*

LOVE IS A FLAWED DANCE

Love is a flawed dance
Some dance her slow and graceful
An intimate waltz,
Safe in the arms of their partner
A feeling of coming home
Her dance could mirror a tango
Full of passionate looks and touches,
Burning fires upon the skin

Love's dance is imperfect
Filled with cruel dance partners,
Stepped-on toes
And dance steps missed
Yet somehow Love prevails,
Finding those who've sworn
That they would dance no more
Catching us off guard
Until suddenly our heels begin
To tap upon the floor

But not all hear Love's silent song;
Her ever-changing rhythm
Forged of skipped heartbeats
And knowing glances
Woven with stolen kisses
And whispered names;
Some aren't even destined
To dance Love at all

—Paige Huntsman, age 12

IN THE WAITING ROOM

Your mother is a small-town dance
that could never find their footing
as she fluttered through wonder
a monsoon of gulps and Parkinson's:

a misdiagnosis, a misstep, more pills,
a misstep, more pills, a mission of: hope
enters the room and pisses in the corner
and punches the person sitting next to you

—*Thomas Fucaloro*

MEMORY

Memory is a silent disguise
that shrouds the darkness in white.
To reminisce is to romanticize—
To recount is to rewrite.

The haze of remembrance exhibits the past
through perfectly tinted rosy glass.
In false recollection and idyllic reverie—
In the name of nostalgia, be his memory.

No, time does not heal—
It simply forgets the pain;
For fondness is easier to feel
than passionate disdain.

—Maria Nikolakakos, age 17

YOU HAVE TO

      beat the well-worn drum of beauty,
even when you're out of time
and everything you make feels slight
or trite or insufficient to the moment.
Play, even when your palms on the skin
of the drum are dry and cracked or
clammy and sweating, and you think *no one,*
no one is listening. Each touch makes its own
music, thumping or clanging through the
shared air, leaping from your hands to other
ears in waves the length of which you can't
control; you can only beat out your own
rhythm, holding the drum between
your knees like an empty bucket, a full bowl,
a burden, a taut-stretched blessing,
the thing that holds you to your mound,
the crowning, drowning sound of Earth.

        —Heidi Mordhorst

MY BODY IS AN OBSTINATE DRUM

I become reacquainted with my body
in sacred loneliness, whole
minutes of hot water to myself.

Hands sticky from self-expression, skin stretched
soft with lavender streaks—I wash the day's (week's?) spit-up
out of what's left
of my split ends and examine

this body. Mine
and not mine,
a rearranged childhood
bedroom. I return to it
every age I've ever been:
a sloppy drunk,
a teenager tender with shame,

but my body
is an obstinate drum
pulsing on with an arguing heart,
hell-bent
on this woman

I'm becoming.

—*Susannah Thorngate-Rein*

YOUR BODY OBSTINATE DRUM

TRYING TO LOVE MYSELF

featuring Andrea Gibson

I am always surprised by the skin that stretches and folds when my fingers move. The lines I trace between my pores. No snow-flake is ever the same but put my hand under the microscope and you will find that my body is a rugged drum, skin stretched over bone. I am the percussionist of my fate. Hit it so hard I pul-verize the ladybugs I see dead on the road. My skin shouts at me about space, how it wants to travel in rockets away from me and I will forever shout back I am trying to love it more than to the moon and back. I hold my hands, feel the dried-out skin that matches my peeling love, my heart is like a blood-orange. I slice it into quarters, then quarter those, it is as my favorite poet said before, *I love you to pieces, too.*

I mean, I try.

That is to say, when my body wishes to be loved I answer with a butcher knife. And when I climb mountains, my being wishes *to become the sky.* Light-blue sweaters will forever hold my wishes in between their woolen threads, the threads that mark my arms and my legs, that make me scared of swimming in public spaces and sometimes by myself too. I don't dare take a bath sometimes out of fear that my scars will turn to life and become the rope I hang myself with.

I mean, I want to live.

Want to see more volcanoes, ashes spreading in the wind.
Want to love the beat that is my heart spreading blood and
vigor from my head to my toes.

Want to go to hot thermal baths, see my skin turn green
in their beauty.
Want to see temples, this time I will be the one praying for
my friends' safe arrival to their new home.

I mean, I want to dance.

—*Kika Man*

FOOLISH

Hope
hears birdsong in a blizzard
plucks adventurous violets
from drought-devastated earth
dances in anticipated rain
under an obdurate sky

An obstinate epiphany
Hope
sports her quixotic cap 'n' bells
dons optimistic motley
celebrates
when sober Common Sense
would sit alone and cry

—*Nancy Cummins Bierman*

HOPE OBSTINATE EPIPHANY

THE BARTENDER

For Shappy

When you found out that a poet in our community
had become homeless, you filled a duffle bag

with old clothes, carefully tucking into every pocket
a travel-size toothpaste or small bar of soap,

deodorant, shampoo, a small comb, and I stood,
confused, telling you to just put them all in a travel bag,

but you said it would preserve pride if it seemed
like an accident, like the items had been forgotten,

and lucky for him, but I pushed back, saying,
In this scenario you've created, you are implying

every time you do laundry, while folding your clothes
you stick a travel-size toiletry in each pocket?

And you thought about it, and shrugged: *Sure, yeah.*
And what was wild in that moment was that

it was believable. You were the type of person
who if someone marched up to you behind the bar

and said, *Hey, I hate bothering you about this, but . . .*
do you have any toothpaste? it would be absolutely

reasonable that you'd pull some out of your pocket
with a delighted grin, as if you had been waiting

all night for just that question. You were just that way:
a delight, a wizard, a reliable lighthouse. Oh love,

your death has been an impossible experiment, showing
every day how easily such wondrous and mysterious gifts

can just disappear, how all that rare and incandescent joy
can simply snuff out once someone like you is gone.

—*Cristin O'Keefe Aptowicz*

MY SOUL IS A BROKEN EXPERIMENT

my soul is a broken experiment
i dipped my hands in my heart
and tore it apart
trying desperately to find the right measurement
of blood and tears
of memories and bottled laughter
of scraped knees and silent screams

my soul is a broken experiment
made up of other failed tests
tried throughout my life

1. how to fit in
   it never worked
   i wasn't made like the rest of them
   i cried too much,
   laughed too loud,
   never understood how to find a man pretty,
   yearned to hold a girl's hand

2. how to look cool
   do i put my hands in my pockets? do i smile? do i smirk?
   i should be laid back
   but i can't stop looking behind my back
   at all the fears that chase me

3. how to find myself
   this is one i'm still working on
   i toss crumpled sheets of mangled words
   in the garbage can
   next to faulty personalities
   and friends i will never get back
   and people i will never be

my soul is a broken experiment
so with guitar-callused hands
i place a band-aid over the cracks

—*Eleanor Coughlin, age 15*

LOVE IS A GENTLE JUNKYARD

Love is a gentle junkyard
Where pretty weeds grow tall,
And thorns strangle anything truly beautiful
It is littered with shreds of hope, trust, and fallen rose petals

It holds the scent of stale, yet sweet perfume
Broken glass
Tattered dress clothes hang, limp
Letters of care and affection are asleep in the fire
An embrace holds the lock on the gate

Old memories lie discarded in the mud
A *Welcome Home* mat, once bright and soft,
Is now coarse and dark
A cloud of betrayal covers the sky

Puddles all around
Denial eats away the truth
Anger fills any leftover space

Because love,
Once a beautiful bloom,
Is now littered with skeletons
And shed skin

—Jesse Whitaker, age 15

HOW I RECALL IT

Memory is a midnight junkyard

distorted with hyperbole,

chrome bits shining, tires overblown,

your heart—an engine thrumming

beneath my steady hand. There was no rust

to chafe the conversation, no dust

settled in your ears or cobwebs

in your lashes, the rats had not yet settled in

to gnaw and claw against my hope,

and that kiss between us

was as smooth as leather

and flush with love

—*Heather Smith Meloche*

THIS IS HOW I LOSE YOU

forgetting is a capricious lens

and death a surreptitious exit
details leave, doves flying the cote

mother-of-pearl buttons sigh
against blue shirting

sound of hangers ringing
in an empty closet

eyeglasses dropped on the dresser
disappear into a drawer, empty of eyes

I look for your shape in fallen leaves
at Parque Olivar, a place we never went

your shadow shrinks at noon
chalk outline, bloodstain on sidewalk

I save your last voicemail
laugh spirals seashell of my ear

photo of us on Cerro San Cristobal
tucked against my ribs still fades to ghost

I look for us from the living side
try to see myself again

—*Aruni Wijesinghe*

THE RETROSPECTOSCOPE

We refract the light of the present
through the desperate lens of our past,
a retrospectoscope
with which we frantically
scrutinize and analyze
sanitize and normalize
summarize and otherwise
organize the words and actions
of millions of people
over seconds and days and decades
of life and death and love and rage
just so we can write another page
in our autobiography,
indelible,
yet in mirror-hand
incomprehensible.

—*Vishesh Jain*

SHAME IS A BURNING MEADOW

Shame is a burning meadow
Destroying the unspent seeds,
the blooming honeysuckle,
the ragged grasses,
with its indiscriminate torch.

It leaves behind the unidentifiable remains
of the wild
and the innocent
scattered in a charred and choked field.

This is no place for growth.

—*Amanda Hoepner*

ISOLATION AND MELODY

Isolation is the human melody
which is to say sweet silence, a lone soliloquy,
a place of peace from all the bustle,
just an echo, just a rustle,
a quiet aria which fills the night,
a slow sonata to sooth our sight.
And as we muster every minute,
it is a momental minuet.
Isolation is human majesty,
which is to say it flows with vigorous victory,
a fermata on full rest,
just one octave above the best,
all empowering and yet alone.
It emphasizes endless mystery
beyond our human frequency.
Isolation describes humanity.

—*Thomas Aaron Pondolfino, age 17*

DOULA

If our mother had met the split-end woman answering phones
in the downtown office as she slipped into a gown,
you could have been nothing but the air evaporating
off the soup she craved in the months after that faceless man
slid out of his wedding ring. Shame swells into her belly until
guilt, that obstinate midwife, gives way to gravity. She expects
punishment for her supposed sin from God, and yet, from her body
emerges you, a definite creature, one with sharp canines
which pierce grapes until they burst with joy. You trespasser,
you lucky bastard, you son-of-a-bitch, you flip quarters
into the fountain and watch them fall into the drain,
and yet here you are, settling. To be the shiny head of Lincoln
swept under the sofa and then later found, to be something
previously unwanted now discovered. And that rainy Thursday,
when you swerved into the one-way street, the pothole
turned your bicycle into metal scrap and your body
into a collection of bruises. Delivered by fire trucks
into the home you were born in, the one where we boil
water for soup and then steep ourselves in forgiveness.

—*Sophia Hall, age 16*

THE WATERMILL, THE GRANDDAUGHTER

What is it that shadows give each other?
—Alejandra Pitzarnik

& the aging chest of my mother. She had 2 boys before me, that have cried for her milk, teethed in her sleep. When I was born, the doctors removed the womb of the woman who gave birth before her, my mother tells me. My name means *hope,* anyway. There is a lake inside a frozen lake off route 79 & when you drive the highway up from South to North Dakota, you'll hear its fish swimming in your engine—that is what it's like to hear my grandmother remember my name: *You have so much joy in you, the light drinks from your lips.* It's okay that this is my cousin's name. My father had a perm in the '80s & my curly hair brings me closer to her memory. She asks, *Wasn't it dark before?* (& I figure we're all like that) I watch my face unfold beneath his beard & his nose, become a stork's child mid-sky of my grandmother's questions. Mother says my legs are my father's & her legs are of hers. I don't mind—when he looks at me, he is reminded of his hometown, its boundless fields. My body can be so distant, sometimes I was never really born here—I know so little of my country. My parents are married now, since '85, & when I send our invites, I imagine grandmother dressed for their wedding: leather shoes & long skirt. The stairs, up to the church, small bathrooms. She asks, *Is he the Englishman?* when my mother tells her I'm engaged. *We'll have Georges in the family. Georges!* she says. Blood makes up about 7 percent of a total body weight—it's more for her: she is this kind of watermill—name one thing as tall as Denver: a quarter of the average depth of an ocean, any family will say this. Dementia sinks into ours & before the knees gave out, I think she did water gymnastics on Tuesdays. Before incontinence pads & beta blockers. In a lake 763 kilometers from London, I hear my heartbeat below water.

That's what it's like when one day, we sit & puzzle in her winter garden, the sun ultrasounds our bodies—the shadow, our impossible midwife, delivering us, shaped like two foeti, not meaning the same thing, when really they do.

—*Nadine Hitchiner*

THE TRUTH IS AN ELUSIVE MIRAGE

The truth is an elusive mirage,
A cascading undulation,
Of the rolling dunes, the sunbaked days
We defy to get to this place
Where an oasis does lie.
The thing we live for.
The hope we forge.
All to come to this point,
Where the nonexistent roads
We travel through life,
Over the ups and downs and the sands of strife,
Converge and diverge all at once.

But the question remains not *whether*
Any creature could survive here,
But how they will transform
In this vast, endless plain, with spirit
That stretches beyond our mind,
Whose sands conceal the true meaning, the oasis of life,
In the folds of its heat and confusion.

But below the surface, we see through the illusion,

Creatures who have found the true oasis,
Not a mirage,
And have adapted,   and changed,   and survived,

Thrive.

—*Trishuli Mandal, age 13*

DONE AND UNDONE

Memory is an obstinate mirror,
A reflected disruption,
What you have done, and what you have left
Undone, in the language of confession.
When you meet at the tangled family reunion of yourselves,
Unbound by temporality,
The past you is ashamed of the future's hollow eyes,
The future blames the past's rash actions,
And the present looks for the exit
       or at least a closet to cry in.
Even as you drive away, rearview vision blurred,
Here comes memory again,
The self interrupting the self,
The nagging child in the backseat of consciousness,
The well-actually of your own voice, echoing
remember remember remember at a speed you can't outrun.
When you pull over to breathe, stumbling out of the car
To your knees, memory joins you,
Tells you to turn over the stone near your hand.
Memory whispers, *What could be under this one?*
You know, but you turn it over anyway,
And it's you, as always, it's you,
in all your accreted muck,
You, in the obstinate mirror of memory.

—*Daniel Roop*

SHARP-EDGED PUZZLE

My father is a broken mirror,
which is to say, he sees himself
in fragments:

part father whose instinct
to patch a cut or punch a problem
is stronger than his instinct to hug,

part widower weeping
when he thinks no one is listening
for the wife he couldn't save,
and for the husband he couldn't be,

part son whose father's love was a razor
of ice that sliced and left no evidence,

part soldier splintered in the jungles
of Vietnam whose youth bled out.

This is all to say, when I look at him,
I see myself, all glass and shine,
when the sun catches my sharp edges.

—*Julene Waffle*

CONTEMPLATION

The past is a broken mirror,
which is to say
that I can see myself in it
but it's not a true reflection
of who I am.

—*Ron Barton*

YOUR BODY IS A FLAWED FUNHOUSE MIRROR

Exiting the *bedroom,* entering the *bathroom.*
Where fake sunlight switched on
as shaking hands grip a shirt's smooth lilac fabric,
lifting to reveal milky skin.
Eyes wander to sneak a peek
You should know this *type of activity is not for the weak.*
What's seen is just a reflection,
Just a body displayed on glass attached to the bathroom wall.
But the mirrors were part of a funhouse,
distorting every angle and shape of your body.
Causing faces to droop from the weight
of an ever-growing double chin,
and stomachs to be thickly textured
like the cheesecake devoured on birthdays.
And you'd think that the body checking was under control.
Until a window became a mirror.
And the gym was suddenly a mirror.
And the grocery store was a mirror.
And work was a mirror.
And home was a mirror.
And your phone was a mirror.
And peers were a mirror.
And school was a mirror.
You become a narcissist but not being full of self,
You become full of hatred.

—*Luka Galle, age 17*

CLOWN COLLAGE

Hope, you feckless party clown, drag your red
clumsy shoes and distorted grinning face;
stuff your endless useless bright stream of dead
exploited worm silk in its hiding place.

You juggle flaming knives and sweet ripe fruit
and spring coiled snakes from dry-roasted nut cans;
you dangle rubber chickens from your suit
pocket and offer elaborate plans.

Cram your insane posse in a wagon,
pop your latex odes to animal joy,
burst the twisted throat of ego's dragon,
and toss my expectations like a toy.

But for hope's wild reckless glory grifting,
Anesthetized guests wait dreamless, drifting.

—Jennifer Gilley

ENTERTAINMENT, SOMEWHERE

Regret is a sad party clown
emerging smudge mouthed
on the birthday of the baby
born convulsing.

The clown's face is pill white
without the need for paint. Pulls rizla
from a purse instead of handkerchiefs,
turns teeth yellow with ta-da.

The clown juggles personalities,
bursts a balloon animal, ties the sag
around its polka dot biceps
and blames someone.

The clown is upsetting the children.

The clown's final act is vanishing
like a septic limb. But first,
the clown performs the meanest
trick of all, calls me *family*,

wants to be paid.

—*Carson Wolfe*

WHAT I ALLOW

Love can be a desperate promise
kept by a long-time junkie with
a cuticle-biting habit. Love can
be a desperate promise that it
won't snort again but again
feels so good and you promise
yourself only once more is love,
true love, is what I allow to kill
me. Desperately. I promise. To.

—*Thomas Fucaloro*

BIRTH OF VENUS

Sandro Botticelli, ~1486, tempura painting, 5'8" x 9'2"

Memory is a human promise I do not see
      the line where my life lives
            I woke fully formed inside

a collection of yellow dresses
      ducks on a string
            peaches in a jar

preserving sweetness for the crumbling
      house What makes me sigh
            & become a woman

waiting in a window as slices of fruit
      turn bruised on a white plate
            I am careful with my totems

the saints hanging
      in a mirror We are waiting for something
            to happen I lose the shape

for a time The line
      manifests in corners,
            shuffles through a crack

to stretch inside a square of light,
      soft belly raised
            to a trembling hand

          —Emily Zogbi

SUFFOCATING PHOENIX

My father is a burning promise.

His lies brand my body,
forever mar my smooth skin.
His truths embody absence,
like carefully handwritten letters set aflame.

My father is a burning promise
and I am the suffocating phoenix.

He promised he would stay,
and I drowned away in the ashes
of naive reveries as, once again,
he went away, away, away.

My father is a burning promise,
and I am the scorching mess he made.

—Kohana Mehl-McKee, age 16

POEM IN WHICH TRAGEDY UNLEARNS MY NAME

and I forget its signature markings: a coding hospital room, the way
sunset digs another grave, silence. Liquidate the bluebonnets

and garnish the gin with baby's breath. I have no need for dying
things anymore so that must be why I'm all alone. Almosts

atrophy between my teeth. Death was never a last-minute
scourge, by which I mean it is an antique

affliction that I've carried in my back pocket. When I turn
it inside out, the dirt designed for caskets devastates the ground

below. My therapist says I make tsunamis out of tidal pools
and it's been so long since saltwater came with a horizon. Last time

I stepped into the ocean, I nearly vertigoed into a sun-spot. I tend
to remember people I have never met best—they come to me

in brilliant streaks of night terrors and stay with me all day.
I swallow pins on a map to forget where I've been without caring

it might take me back there someday. If the apocalypse begins,
who will come running and how will they know where to go?

I try not to ask too many questions these days. It's not that curiosity
doesn't call, I just can't take the silence they bring with them.

Did you find my name in a take-a-number dispenser and forget
to throw it out when you got what you needed?

You know I'm nothing but bones and calamity these days.
Show some grace, give me mercy. Say my name doesn't sit

bitter in your mouth like the stems of dandelions
swaying at the base of a long-forgotten gravestone.

—*Erica Abbott*

THE PLAYGROUND CIRCUS

I am a broken sideshow
to the girls in the playground
who sweep my fringe upwards
and spit laughter as they measure
my forehead with their fingers,
counting up to my crown,
declaring me a seven-head.

They treat me like a clown
entertaining a cruel audience,
I don't want to be branded
a *crybaby,* so I hold back
my tears.

These girls who embarrass me,
do not see me the way I see them,
ordinary, normal, regular.

What hurts the most is the ringleaders
of the schoolyard circus
are my best friends.

—May Wolfe, age 10

PAY YOUR MONEY

Love is a sideshow
           you are the barker
I'm the bearded lady
waving your cane, you cry

          love for sale
               barely used
          a handed-down love
          reduced 50% for the next 24 hours

I touch your faded passion
          torn at the corners
          raggedy and thin
pay your money and move along

          —Judith Duncan

MY MOTHER LIKES TO TALK ABOUT MY BIRTH

How I hid, wrinkled and damp, under the milk-white
      dome of her belly.
How they cut her open like a fish to hoist me out
      a month too soon, my
lung collapsed like a wet envelope, an ulcer the size
      of a tarnished silver
dollar flaming inside my abdomen. She likes to talk
      about the blood,
an endless stream of red scarves being pulled
      from her cavity by a cruel
magician, my birth a midnight sideshow, all that crimson
      set against the
sterile linoleum floor, against the drifts of snow
      painting the windows
white, shuddering us in. A baby born in winter,
      so close to the birth of
Jesus, they called me a Christmas miracle.
      An untouchable gift, wrapped in
gauze, ribboned with tubes and kept in a translucent box
      until my lungs
opened like the mouth of a flytrap. But mostly,
      she likes to ask what thanks
I've given for the privilege of being here; what debts
      I have paid for the
cruelty of almost costing her her life.

—*Sheleen McElhinney*

ADHD

The mind is a divided sideshow.
It is crowded, running in different directions,
obscure and shrouded, living in wild curations.
My thoughts are a sideshow, forgettable and intrusive,
forever infamous and elusive.

—Isaiah Griffith, age 15

THE MIND DIVIDED SIDE SHOW

I AM A SILENT SONGBIRD

i am a silent songbird; that doesn't mean i cannot sing
doesn't mean i have no rhythm or that i am not brimming
with melodies and lyrics tucked away under my wings,
stories dripping from my tongue like water falling from a spring
i shout to the wind and sky, ask them why they're so far from me;
i am a silent songbird with songs nobody is hearing

i love to listen to other birds; i admire their bright chirping,
the way that they can flap their wings and speak without ever holding
back—my songs have a bitter taste while theirs are sweet
because i will never understand how they can so freely bleat
i will never enjoy a song as a freestyle, nor a speech
because i will never be sure enough that i will sing and not screech

what good is a songbird who doesn't sing, an artist who never draws,
and what good is a performer who only sings to their walls?
i am an audience member waiting for my chance up on the stage,
but when i find myself at the mic, i cannot speak without chains
i have so much to say, so many words bubbling in my throat,
but i am a silent songbird, and so my mouth remains closed

—*E. J. Warren, age 16*

LOVE IS AN ELUSIVE SONGBIRD

he had an affinity for songbirds
him with his teary blue eyes, blue like the sky after a weary sunrise
and his voice like honey candies, melting you and drawing you closer

Why do you keep them in cages? I asked him once
and the corner of his mouth twitched, his ring finger
      reaching out to caress a blue beauty
Darling, it's so they don't fly away. Simple.

And as I stood outside of his cages, his silver- and gold-laden
disguises
I felt his hands reach for mine, encircling me
      in blue softness and sweet sayings
until I became part of his collection, his treasures, his silent followers

Is it wrong for me to worship you? He asked me once
and I laughed and shook my head, knowing deep down
      that it was I who worshiped him
I'm nothing worth worshiping. I'm only human.

He drew me in so that all I could see was the blue
      of his veins and vision,
the blue that he so easily traced across my being,
      charming me and praising me and ensnaring me
until I collapsed in a cage painted blue like the sky
      before sunset, a pitiful rendition of life

What am I to you? I asked him for the final time
as his trophies fell silent and the orange light of day vacated his space
You are my favorite, of course. You are my love.

And even as I pulled my hand away from his,
      cold fingers releasing mine with ease
the shadows of those blue bars still followed me,

encased me, swallowed me
so that I was still his, even after the death
of our miserable attempt at affection

What do I even want? I asked myself one night
as the sky hid behind clouds and the moon wept for all of her stars
I want to be free again. I don't want to live as his lost prize.

He was no longer the one I wanted to adore,
but the one I wanted to forget
him with his pains and frustrations and sweetness,
him with his half-smile and gentle hands
the hands with which he crafted inescapable houses and empty places

Was this love worth the chase? I could imagine him whispering
and I sighed and shook my head, cage of dusty blue
flickering around me
Darling, this is not love. Simple.

—*Amanda Aiyu Lee, age 17*

HEIRLOOM

My father ripens like an heirloom
on the vine—skin sagging and collecting
sunspots as he grows plumper.

I wonder if my father still sings
lullabies to the lettuce each night.
If he still tracks their growth

on a ruler. Still cradles
his favorite ficus between
his fingertips. If he still bathes

each leaf, on both sides, lathers
them with a toothbrush. If he still
raises them with such excruciating

devotion. I wonder if he will cry
when he hears my poem
about his garden—like how he wept

when the foxes ate his chicory.
If his heart still patters like June rain
on a tin roof or if he watches over

his nursery, quiet as a pair of
socks. If he will ever quench
his hunger for a perfect heirloom

tomato. My father is a mad songbird with a garden full of well-worn, passed-down

promises.

—*Yoda Olinyk*

POETRY IS A DESPERATE SONGBIRD

Poetry is a desperate songbird craving
spring in winter's apex. My heart speaks

to me in canary
'til it's blue all over. Forgive me

while I bleed my little tragedies—
the arm that split in the middle;

the needles that push-pinned
the anxiety of coming apart

at the joint into my bones;
a patchwork cervix;

a grandfather's embalmed nose
cresting glistened coffin;

every man who swallowed
my yellow-feathered intuition

and left my soot lungs caved in.
I have dug my fingernails black

out of the coal mine rubble—
an ex who still infiltrates

every inbox hungry for a voice box
to bite; a mother who still can't unravel me

from my jeans size; a cervix plucked
of every dysplastic cell. I have tipped

myself like an inkwell, cantillated
tar out of every exit wound

in fevered hymn. I have sung and sung
and sung my barricaded throat

abraded but dislodged.
Every poem is one last molted,

onyx-dipped plume sacrificed
for truth. I hold every winter

like a breath in my lungs, wait
for the starling's trachea to bloom.

—Kait Quinn

MIXED-DRINK MELODY

My memory
is a siren song of faults.
My legs have known
hangover ache,
a mixed-drink melody
of unseen sapphire and wine
bruise.
a wounded pride
that never stopped me
stumbling
back to the bar.
The gallons of beer
never sang *stop,*
no barstool
ever screamed
at my heaviness.
The past
is a mad songbird.
It may never again
be able to sing
its grief into my ears.

—*James Roach*

(SUPER)HERO

Hope is
a bootleg superhero—
Bare chested with
a dad bod, wearing
last summer's unwashed
beach towel as a cape,
with thrift store acid-washed
jeans too skinny for
public comfort.
Hope remains
unbothered by
your averted eyes,
or your whispered
critiques regarding
his fashion choices.

Hope has
no secret identity
or esoteric lair;
he lives within
the realm of everyday,
and takes the city bus,
paying his fare
with coins removed
from the jingling
cacophony of a
nylon fanny pack.

Hope is not rich.
Unlike some of
those other superheroes.
But Hope is real.
Unlike all of
those other superheroes.

Hope never arrives to rescue.
He is always there with you,
hugging your soul
when you need it most.

—*Sidney Jones, Jr.*

AN OPEN LETTER TO HOPE

Traitor.
Here I am again,

in my hospital room, folded
over like a tablecloth. You swore

you would stay
this time. I can't forgive you

for coming back.
Oh hope, you craven superhero.

You grab the knife
out of my fingers.

You spoon cereal
into the dish

of my mouth.
You bind this throat

with honesty like trust
is a priest.

You disappear
into the fog so many times,

I think the fog is you.
You take on the persona

of my mother
when I am orphaned

of any courage.
Here, where the doctor left

me alone with a starving belly
and fifteen hundred grams

of guilt, you dared forgive
this body

for not being brave.

—*Toby Grossman*

THE MIND IS A BROKEN THUNDERSTORM

The mind is a broken thunderstorm.
It is never still.
It booms and bangs and is rarely quiet.
It clouds up, and in the darkness
you do things you regret.
It can shoot sharp words out like lightning
and make loved ones seek shelter.
Sometimes it feels like it will never stop.
And it may not.
The mind is a broken thunderstorm.

—Astrid Roop, age 11

IRRITABLE BOWEL SYNDROME (I.B.S.)

My body is a capricious thunderstorm,
which is to say
a furious-food-fleeting-feeling, sharp and stinging, coming
from my core
confusing

a brutal blizzard
barbarous, not marvelous
manic, messy

a militant monsoon
but others can't feel the pain in the rain
or know how hard the blast can blow

anytime, anywhere
she doesn't care if I'm
sitting, walking, running
drained, disfigured, distressed
worn from the storm

the pain persists so I resist

after several seasons, I still seek the reasons
what causes my storm to start?

all I can answer is
battling with the bowel requires
grit, grace, and
Guts.

—*Becca Howard, age 15*

MY GUILT IS A GLORIFIED TROPHY

My guilt is a glorified trophy
I keep it up high on my shelf
I sometimes pretend to ignore it
but I'm proud that I earned it myself

My guilt is a glorified trophy
I never show off that it's there
but I shine it and dust underneath it
I pick it up gently with care

My guilt is a glorified trophy
it's not really metal, I know
it's shiny, but it's only plastic
there's a chip on the corner that shows

My guilt is a glorified trophy
it's old—from 2005
but I still have it and I still see it

I think that it might be alive

My guilt is a glorified trophy
I steal glances at my windowsill
and though no one asks how I got it
I secretly hope that they will

My guilt is a glorified trophy
it still holds its cheap silver shine
it's there and it sits and I see it
it's mine and it's mine and it's mine

—*Faith Manary*

PARTICIPATION TROPHY

The past is a well-worn trophy—
and while some sneer
at the word "participation,"
I am amused by the accusation,
knowing how I
slogged through
the ditch of my darkest days
until my boots filled with
water & my brow
creased with sorrow
and I refused to drown.

—*William Polking*

TIME IS AN UNSPOKEN TROPHY

Time is an unspoken trophy,
a silver cup that
grows both heavier
and more empty
over the years.
It's engraved
with a name
you've forgotten,
awarded for a feat
no longer possible.
The hands
of the clock
reach out
to congratulate you.

—Jessica Swafford

FEATHERWEIGHT CHAMPION

You're killing yourself
                              for the blue ribbon
of your limbs   like your body   is a hard-won trophy,
                    the chalice
                              of your clavicle
                                        a medal.

In the hospital, over supervised meals of cornflake packets
and full fat

                    milk, we promised
each other we would recover.
                                        Why did you lie?

Your last meal   was a month ago.
Darling, you don't have to   hollow
                    your bones into a cave
                              for the echo
                    of your voice.

                                        I hear you.
Every time you text me
that you are too angel   to eat, I spill
the spoon of my soup into a goblet.
                    I am a procession at your funeral
and this is my eulogy. Can I stop
dying now please?
I don't know how to live

in the tender skin
of forgiveness
while you cleave your ribs
into a diamond
polished for Hunger's crown.

              If I am a ghost
will your slipping away   haunt me less?

I plant care   in a wing so you shouldn't be afraid
      of its weight.

If a casket   is the only victory
you will claim,   here, my body is yours.
I will triumph it into lack
and you can call me   grave.

      —*Toby Grossman*

GOOD GUYS

The last time I saw you alive, you hovered in my doorway,
the screen door flapping against your shoulder, flies
I'd have to kill later whirring through, landing on the apples
in the fruit bowl, preening themselves in the sun.
I didn't want you going back to that rented room above
the bar; filthy cot, deadbolts on the door to keep the thieves
out, piss stains in the hallway. *Why don't you stay* I said,
your motorcycle leaning bored in the driveway as if to say
You coming or what? You flicked your lit Marlboro
onto my neighbor's lawn, shifted your weight,
my hospitality like too much sun on the back of the neck.
Those guys over there are my friends. We grew up with a
lot of those guys. Good guys. I know the ones
you mean. Toothless now as they were at eight, setting fire
to the trash cans, running barefoot from the cops, commiserating
over absent fathers inside sheet-metal forts. All of you lost boys,
your dreams carved out with switchblades. Your past like a glorified
wasteland—your memory, a burning compass.

—*Sheleen McElhinney*

HEIRLOOM

My mother is a handed-down wedding gown.
Bridal train tarnished by a lineage of women
who flinched at keys turning a lock.

For her sweet sixteenth, she wanted to drench
her new denim jeans in the bathtub,
wear them in sunlight until they dried tighter
than her lover's grip.

Instead, whisky fists showered her with shards
of confetti. Her days spinning like The Specials
on vinyl, the chorus, *too much too young,*
a personal hymn.

These lyrics, a serenade for a runaway,
a girl cut loose from the father of the baby
born before she was old enough to sip champagne.

She tailored herself to new suitors, repeated
I do, I do, I do. It was my mother who taught me
to patchwork in black and blue.

My mother, a choir of, *this is just what men do,*
he didn't hurt you worse than I've been through.
Now I am a handed-down wedding gown,
sipping from the same underage flute.

Church pews stacked with women
who stare absently at the daughter
crowded in my abdomen. The zip
drawn all the way up to my throat.
He tightens,

I choke.

—*Fae Wolfe*

ACKNOWLEDGEMENTS AND NOTES

The Jeditors are grateful for the hundreds of submissions we received this year, especially from the teachers who submitted for several of their students. Every poem was read multiple times, and the top 200 were passed along by a diverse armada of volunteer first readers who themselves took several weeks to arrive at their selections: Jason H. S. Nadelbaum, Tiffany Woodley, Grace Coe, Janet Fagal, Charles Childers, Kathy Amburgey, Daniela Aguilar, Katie Leach, Samantha Sugar, Robert Yelley, Janine DeBaise, Jade P. Albert, Nicole Gil, Rudra Bach, and Jamey Austin.

Thanks to all the photographers and designers who contributed to this project in one way or another: Peter Dressel, Jamie Kleiman, Cristina Gómez, Natasha Janardan, Emily Van Cook, Amy Law, Lindsay Lake. And to Tanesha Nicole Tyler, the Jeditors' editor and associate publisher at Button Poetry, thank you for keeping us all on track.

The silent partner at Metaphor Dice is Oliver Wellington, who was also a member of Taylor Mali's eighth-grade English class at Cape Cod Academy in the mid-1990s.

Last, to the countless poets and teachers who have used Metaphor Dice in the past or helped to hawk them at a conference or contributed a lesson plan or activity to these pages, among them Sharon Olds, Mark Doty, Dorianne Laux, Brendan Constantine, Danusha Laméris, Joseph Millar, Seema Reza, Eric Guerrieri, Margaret Simon, Tiffany Woodley, Kai Coggin, Popsy Kanagaratnam, Megan Falley, Mike McGee, and Andrea Gibson.

LESSON PLANS AND APPENDICES

WHICH IS TO SAY

Which Is To Say was for many months the working title of this anthology. Of course, it's another way of saying *in other words* or *what I'm really saying is,* but it's also an extremely useful tool for linking together two phrases in a poem, one perhaps a little too creative to be clear, the other perhaps too clear to be creative. The phrase *which is to say* operates the same way a poem does as a whole: *It's another way of saying something, making an observation, or simply speaking your truth.* Poetry is the tool we reach for when we know what we want to say, but not how to say it or if it can even be put into words. If it were possible to say something simply—to say it without context in a single phrase—we wouldn't need to put it in a poem. We would just blurt it out like a child who has learned a new curse.

Poetry exists at the intersection of truth and fact. On the surface these seem like synonyms but to an emotional linguist they are parallel sentiments. Fact is immutable, concrete, and indifferent. Truth is messy, emotional, and honest. They are different ways of trying to get at what matters but they rarely touch. *Which is to say* is one of the most flexible ropes that can bind these two together. Which is to say, this is how we explore our world, our minds, and our truths. Maybe it's the *only* way anyone will remember our truth.

Which is to say, you have probably seen the phrase *which is to say* many times in this book.

—*Jared Singer*

THE WEAPONS

No touching. No pens. No pencils over three inches or they will be confiscated as weapons.

I was asked to teach a workshop at a women's prison by Murphy Anne Carter, director of the Freehand Arts Project for the jail just outside of Austin, Texas. I asked Cristin O'Keefe Aptowicz to join me. On more than one occasion, I've spent a few miserable hours in military jail (whiskey, sucker punches), but I've only ever been to a *real jail* to visit someone else. So this was my first glimpse from the inside. I've always known it was a brutal construct, but only in theory. The stark yellow concrete, the nothingness of the dead lawns, the lonely air, the lack of art and life. Jail feels cruel. And it feels like someone is getting off on that cruelty.

There were about twenty women in our class, ranging in age from 19 to about 60. I taught them first about the use of poetry and the way it can pinpoint feelings. I taught about the usefulness of surprise and creativity in your writing. After I had them *declare themselves as poets,* the next step was to flush out an idea and then add unforgettable metaphors. I showed them third-level thinking in metaphor construction.

1. *I like your eyes. They are blue. You seem distant.*
2. *Your eyes are cold blue glaciers. I am always sleeping by the fire.*
3. *Your eyes, blue glaciers that my warmth cannot penetrate.*

They asked questions. We laughed a lot. And then they started writing. Rough drafts about regret. Things they missed, especially good food. Nail salons missed. Love missed. Rough, erotic stuff. Vulnerable stuff about kids. The feels unfurled and the tears started to wash on in.

I then chose a few to roll some Metaphor Dice after they had their rough concepts in poetic form. They would roll:

HAPPINESS / IMPOSSIBLE / PROMISE
Happiness is an impossible promise.

I said, "Raise your hand if you can tweak this idea and load it into your poem?" Too many hands went up. Okay, how about this:

I AM / BACKHANDED / KISS.
I am a backhanded kiss.

They all laughed, and the rest raised their hands. And they began to load their poems with the metaphor ammo. I told them they could place the metaphor up top, in the middle, tweak it, or make it their closer. Almost everyone was eager to share their rough drafts. Cristin and I took turns pointing out lines that could be tightened, and the class took notes. Attentive, ready, and lit up.

Director Carter reported later that one inmate said, "It's so good to feel like you're not incarcerated, even if it's just for an hour." She said everything in the jail is structured and regimented and rulebound. Jail is meant to make everyone feel small and powerless. "But these poetry workshops help them tap into their humanity again. Thank you for coming."

They put together an anthology of the work they had revised and called it *Jail Fat.* Strangers on Kickstarter funded it, and the inmates cried when they found out that people on the outside— people they had never met—thought about them and cared. One final note: The women taking the class had been told by the guard to stay away from me. Nevertheless—and I hope this doesn't get anyone in trouble—after the workshop, one by one, they all gave me a hug on the way back to their cells. And it seemed as if the guard sort of looked the other way to let this happen. Later, I remember sitting in the room with Cristin and Director Carter and just breaking down, so grateful to have been reminded what poetry can do.

—*Derrick C. Brown*

EARLY MISTAKES WITH METAPHOR DICE

The very first Metaphor Dice that I used with students (in the spring of 2016) were printed on paper in my home office in three colors. Before any of them could be used, however, they needed to be filled in by hand, individually cut out using a pair of scissors that was always in demand, creased, folded, and finally taped together. This all took far longer than *the single class period* I had allotted for the task. That was mistake number one.

Mistake number two was thinking that the only way to increase the number of words in play was to make the dice have more sides. I tried 10-sided decahedrons, 12-sided dodecahedrons, and even 20-sided icosahedrons. And then I spent hundreds of hours trying to figure out what all those polyhedrons looked like *flattened out* into two dimensions and how best to arrange three of these shapes on a single sheet of paper. They were great fun, but because my directions and examples were printed on the back, they always got destroyed when the dice were created.

It took me far too long to realize that a better way to increase the number of words in play was to increase the number of *dice*, not the number of sides on the dice. *Besides*, said a friend of mine early on in the project, *throwing a handful of dice feels a little dangerous, but holding a D20 just makes me feel like a seventh grader rolling for charisma points.*

Mistake number three was using paper in the first place. Whatever the shape, the dice were always delicate and easily crushed. That's why I started collecting them in a shoebox at the end of every class and then handing them out again the next day. My students that semester discovered that the only thing better than rolling metaphors from words they had carefully chosen was doing the exact same thing using words that *someone else* had carefully chosen. In the end, the dice became acrylic and were engraved with words I painstakingly chose over the course of a year in consultation with many other writers.

To this day, I still think of words like QUARRY that I wish I had included. The dice offer JUNKYARD as an object, but I now think it would have made a better adjective. Which is to say, this is all evidence that we will have to produce another set of Metaphor Dice in the *junkyard quarry of the not-too-distant future.*

—*Taylor Mali*

FINALLY GETTING IT RIGHT

I have been using Metaphor Dice in my classroom for years now. I was one of the first to "test them out," and I think they're definitely a valuable resource. However, at least in the beginning, the results often fell short of my hopes and expectations. The dice are not a magic wand that will suddenly turn all students into amazing poets. Mine often got stuck on the idea of the rolled metaphor. Then they would shut down during the writing process. Or else they simply jammed the metaphor into a separate poem where it didn't really fit.

But like many teachers, I fine-tune my lessons every year, and during the pandemic I found a strategy that worked. I was teaching a hybrid class—some students in class, others remote—and midway through my lesson, the school's WiFi went down, and we had an hour to kill without computers. I grabbed a set of Metaphor Dice from my desk and did some rolls with the four in-person students. In doing so, I realized the disconnect that my students had been having with my approach: Because they had no experience with workshops in general, they didn't understand *what to do with the metaphor* after they chose one that spoke to them.

Over the course of the hour, I worked with them to better understand how a metaphor is used to create multiple potential meanings at once. I put a single metaphor roll on the board and we all took turns adding specific details that worked to support the comparison. The experience was laid back, creative, and rewarding for the small group. As we continued playing, the students were laughing, clapping, and snapping for the ideas they liked best.

Now that my classes are fully in person again, I have a lesson that works. I start with a song they know that uses metaphors and work with them to break down the various meanings implied by the comparison. After that, we transition to the Metaphor Dice formula (concept = adjective + object) using fill-in-the-blanks, and students volunteer lines that justify or demonstrate the metaphor. Together, we identify the strengths of each metaphor as well as their justifications and make suggestions for improvement. Finally, the students get to play with the dice themselves. Not only do they roll the dice and craft the metaphors, but they are also ready and eager to come up with interesting and creative justifications.

—*Tiffany Woodley*

METAPHOR DICE IN A HIGH SCHOOL CLASSROOM

Lesson length: 1–3 class periods depending on length (about two hours total)

Materials: At least one set of Metaphor Dice, projector/document camera (to share rolls) or one loud student.

Prior Knowledge: Students should know the difference between *abstract* and *concrete* nouns and have had some exposure to figurative language.

Common Core Standards: W3.A, W3.C, W3.D, W.4, W.5[1]

Do Now: Complete three of the following sentences to create *figurative* statements (clearly not *literal*).

1. The night was as dark as . . .
2. Anxiety is like a . . .

---

1 3. Write narratives to develop real or imagined experiences or events using effective technique, well-chosen details, and well-structured event sequences. a) Engage and orient the reader by setting out a problem, situation, or observation and its significance, establishing one or multiple point(s) of view, and introducing a narrator and/or characters; create a smooth progression of experiences or events. c) Use a variety of techniques to sequence events so that they build on one another to create a coherent whole and build toward a particular tone and outcome (e.g., a sense of mystery, suspense, growth, or resolution). d) Use precise words and phrases, telling details, and sensory language to convey a vivid picture of the experiences, events, setting, and/or characters. 4. Produce clear and coherent writing in which the development, organization, and style are appropriate to task, purpose, and audience. (Grade-specific expectations for writing types are defined in standards 1–3 above.) 5. Develop and strengthen writing as needed by planning, revising, editing, rewriting, or trying a new approach, focusing on addressing what is most significant for a specific purpose and audience.

3. The fallen leaves danced like . . .
4. My dreams are . . .

Share out a few examples and fine-tune them as needed.

Step 1: Play a song clip that highlights figurative language and have students discuss in pairs or small groups the various meanings that come from the figurative lines. Suggested songs: "Spirits" by The Strumbellas, "Firework" by Katy Perry, "Girl on Fire" by Alicia Keys.

Step 2: Introduce Metaphor Dice. Say, *This tool uses a formulaic approach for the creation of metaphors in which* **a concept** = **an adjective** + **an object**. *The red, white, and blue dice work together to create metaphors in which "big things" (like abstract nouns or complicated ideas) are equated to "small things" (concrete nouns or more tangible objects) modified by adjectives.*

Work as a whole class to complete the metaphor *without* the dice:

Love is a/an _____ _____
CONCEPT   ADJECTIVE   NOUN

Example: *Love is a favorite toy.*

Ask the class to add meaning by "justifying" the metaphor. In what ways is this statement true? If necessary, prompt them to draw connections with questions such as *How do you treat your favorite toy? What do you do with your favorite toy when you're young? What about when you're older? Toys often have different parts: What are the different parts of love?*

Step 3: Provide students with a list of the words from the RED dice or read them off to the whole class. Have students select one big concept that they will write about.

Step 4: Have students make a list of the concrete words from the BLUE dice that they believe best connect to the selected concept. This can be done by rolling as a class or in small groups depending on how many sets you have in your classroom.

Step 5: Have students select the same number of adjectives from the WHITE dice as they have concrete words from the BLUE.[2]

Step 6: Have students consider the words they've chosen and their feelings regarding the larger concept. With a bigger understanding in mind, ask students to create one stanza for each of the metaphors they want to include. Students should work to select, order, and justify their metaphors with specific details in a way that makes sense for the larger meaning.

Editing (extra period): Students can work in pairs or small groups to share what they create with each other and guess/discuss what larger meanings the author intended. Students should work to improve the order, wording, and specific details of the poem with the larger meaning in mind. This period is also an opportunity to meet with students one-on-one regarding their creations.

—*Tiffany Woodley*

---

2 If you have kids working in groups and want to add a twist, either have them work together to discuss appropriate adjectives or have one student select for another.

METAPHOR (D)ICEBREAKER ACTIVITY

Even though I have been teaching for over twenty years, I still scramble to find an activity to do on the first day that will set the tone for the course as well as our interactions. This activity makes the first day fun and opens the journey for students to fine-tune their words and voices in a supportive environment.

Lesson length: One period

Materials: Enough Metaphor Dice for each student to have one of each color.

Step 1: Put into a box *exactly as many dice as you have students.* If that total is divisible by three, make the number of red, white, and blue dice be equal. If not, throw in some extra white dice (or blue if you need to).

Step 2: As students enter the class, have them grab one die (the color doesn't matter).

Step 3: Once everyone has one die, provide them with the following instructions to choose one *word* on the die:

- If you have a RED die, select a *concept* you think a lot about.
- If you have a WHITE die, select an *adjective* that describes you best.
- If you have a BLUE die, select an *object* that is significant to you.

Step 4: Have students mingle and split into groups of three with one word from each color represented in the group in a way that they think fit well together. If your class isn't divisible by three, one group could include one extra student—the white dice can be added easily—as an extra/alternative.

Step 5: Once students are in their groups, have them share with each other why they chose the words they did and give them some time to get to know each other.

Step 6: To complete the activity, have the students work together to combine their words into a single metaphor and justify it in a way that rings true for all group members. It does not have to be explained in terms of which person chose which word, but the group should agree on the explanation.

Examples: *Social media is a rugged touchdown. In photos, it looks wonderful and exciting. But we can see the frayed edges, the twitch of the smile, the grass and grit, the questioning look, the self-doubt.*

Your mother is a reluctant songbird. Which is to say, she never wanted the spotlight or the solo. She says, "That's why I had you."

My class is all about helping students find their voices, and this activity is a very gentle introduction because no one feels entirely responsible for the metaphor, just an anonymous part of it. If you have time or would like to follow up on the activity, the students can explain their thought process from word selection through to justification of the metaphor.

—*Tiffany Woodley*

FRIDAY ONE-MINUTE METAPHORS

If you've ever taken a good look at the Common Core Standards, you may note that figurative language standards run through all grade levels. For example:

- Third grade: Determine the meaning of words and phrases as they are used in a text, distinguishing literal from nonliteral language.
- Fourth grade: Explain the meaning of simple similes and metaphors (e.g., as *pretty as a picture*) in context.
- Seventh grade: Determine the meaning of words and phrases as they are used in a text, including figurative and connotative meanings.

Teaching students to recognize figurative language can start at a very young age. Think of a toddler joyfully stirring absolutely nothing in a bowl with a stick and saying, "I cooking." We adults love to play along.

I enjoy creating a playful atmosphere when it comes to teaching metaphors. At the end of a long week, students look forward to Friday Game Day. Prompted by my classroom set of Metaphor Dice, one of my sixth graders created a game. She suggested that we roll a single metaphor and all write about the same one. We added a time element to it and called it One-Minute Metaphors, and the game was on! The timer set. Roll the dice. Everyone writes, even the teacher. After the timer went off, we'd each share what we had written.

The winning part was subjective and not truly competitive. We would discuss why we liked each poem and why some worked better than others. I modeled "I vote for A because she included onomatopoeia."

Roll again. Timer set. Write. We'd play as many rounds as time allowed.

Metaphors, like puzzles, challenge students to think on a higher level, to reflect meaningfully, making sense of words that may stretch our perspective in strange ways. Like those creative exercises that ask a student to transform a drawn line into an image, I like how Metaphor Dice encourage out-of-the-box thinking and creative processing. For example, a roll of HEART + DESPERATE + KISS may at first seem to be the stuff of a romantic comedy, but Katie, one of my sixth graders, turned it inward with this poem about loving oneself.

> THE HEART IS A DESPERATE KISS
>
> It wants to feel loved and soon learns,
> after relying too much on others for love,
> that it needs you and only you
> to feel loved.
> And it can be broken,
> broken into a million pieces, but only you
> can make the decision to fix it.

We also made personal connections, which helped to build a classroom community. Jaden showed us that he prefers to spend time alone when writing about how his home can be a kind of "reluctant dance."

> Home is a reluctant dance
> twist and turns
> shakes and shimmies
> hallways of beats and rhythm
> while you hide away from all of that
> to sit in your room and do nothing

Not every roll produced brilliant poetry, but that's not the point. The point is to play with words and stretch perspective, to look at situations with a new lens, and perhaps create something worth sharing and developing a little more. "You should post that one on the class blog!" was the highest praise given in the metaphor dice game.

—*Margaret Simon*

(UN)COMMON METAPHORS

Metaphor the Win

A Vaguely Competitive Writing Game for 3+ Players

Materials needed
- *9 Metaphor Dice (3 red, 3 white, 3 blue)*
- *One regular "numbered" six-sided die*
- *3x5 index cards*
- *Writing utensils*
- *Timer*

Setup & Start
Everyone gets a writing utensil and a stack of index cards. Each player rolls the numbered die, and the highest roller becomes Player 1, who will *control the table* for the first turn. After each turn, play moves clockwise.

Game Length
One *round* of play includes as many *turns* as there are players. Five players would play five turns in a round. A five-player game could take as long as 30–40 minutes for the first round. Consider this before play begins and agree on how many rounds you will play. However, subsequent rounds could be played in considerably less time if needed.

GAMEPLAY FOR TURN 1

Crafting the Common Metaphor
Player 1, who will control the table for the first turn, randomly selects one die of each color and rolls them, arranging the dice in any order they like. They then read the dice aloud and decide on the *Common Metaphor* by inserting whatever connective words they see fit between the dice as needed. Every player—including

Player 1—then writes this exact phrase (called the *Common Metaphor*) somewhere on their own index card. Player 1 then rolls the six-sided die to determine how many additional lines are to be written. For example, if a 3 is rolled then three lines must be added to the Common Metaphor to create a four-line poem. Lines can be added before or after the Common Metaphor. Poems cannot be shorter than two lines (if 1 is rolled) or longer than seven lines (if 6 is rolled) and are further limited by the space on a single side of the index card.[1]

Writing Phase
Player 1 sets the timer for a maximum of three minutes and starts it. During this time all players write a poem of the specified length on their index card. *Be sure to write legibly, because your poem will be read by someone else!* When finished, each player turns their card face down in front of them. All writing must stop when the time is up.

Reading Phase
Player 1 collects and shuffles all cards, then lays them face down and writes a large different letter on the back of each one (A, B, C, etc.). Player 1 picks up and reads aloud the poem on the back of each card and returns it to its original face-down position. Each player should keep track of the letter of their favorite poem. Once all cards have been read—twice if necessary—and are all face down, Player 1 points to each card and asks all players to cast one vote for their favorite poem. Player 1 tallies the votes for each poem on the back of each card. All cards are returned to the players. Did anyone vote for their own poem? That's perfectly legal, but it's risky, especially if the poem received all the votes in that turn! (See *The I in Team Penalty* below.) Turn 2 now begins with Player 2 controlling the table.

---

1 What constitutes "a line of poetry"? Can the Common Metaphor be only half a line? Or must it always count as its own line? How should line breaks be marked and counted? These are all good questions you will have to answer for yourselves as you play!

Scoring

At the end of the round, players add up all of their points, and the player with the most points wins. Unless . . .

The I in Team Penalty!

At the end of the round, a coin is flipped. If it is heads, then any player whose poem received a unanimous score (e.g. 4/4, 6/6), meaning they voted for their own poem, *loses 2 points* for each instance. If it is tails, then no scores change for that round.

Final Thoughts

This game can be a sword to the heart of writer's block, and it often produces great discussions about poetry, metaphor, structure, and the writing process! Those discussions should continue long after the game is over. Be sure to save your favorite cards from the game to revisit with your journal later. Or trade them. Or fold them into airplanes and let them fly where they will!

—Mighty Mike McGee

STANDARD METAPHOR DICE STUDY PLAN

For middle school to retirement

Prior to meeting your class, roll *only* the red and white dice and save the result. As soon as everyone is seated, explain that you will forgo introductions for the moment and jump right into a *free write*. Using a chalk board or similar medium, display your red and white roll as an incomplete sentence. For example: *Love is a broken . . .*

Say, "I'm giving you only part of a sentence. For the next five minutes, please finish the sentence and keep writing. Don't worry about writing a poem. Don't worry about having to share. And PLEASE don't worry about it being any good." After five minutes, have them set aside their writing. If anyone asks to share, assure them there will be a chance a little later.

Why did we just do that? I like to think of the imagination as a kitchen drawer, perpetually crammed with stuff we think we might need later. If your home is anything like mine, when you finally do need something, it's chaos in there: old pens, stiff rubber bands, part of a Happy Meal toy, total bedlam. And as you dig, hoping to recognize what you want, you soon realize that you will have to remove a few things. And they will have to come all the way out. The same is true of our first free-writing prompt; we're uncovering the good stuff.

Of course, some in the group may create amazing first drafts, tapping into the muse right away. Just as likely, there will be a few who are already rethinking their afternoons. To them I would offer this equalizing fact: No matter how accomplished a writer you may be, no matter if you maintain a trophy shelf and your name graces the thresholds of national libraries, one thing will always be true: *Your worst writing lies ahead of you.* So take a deep breath, remember that we are all equal in this classroom, and trust your creativity.

You may now formally start your class with introductions for the day and what's to come. Say, "We're going to write a bunch of poems with a little help from Metaphor Dice!"

Offer up your box of Metaphor Dice and explain how they work. This would also be a good time to review your own understanding of how metaphors themselves operate.1 Personally, I tend to treat metaphor as not merely a descriptive tool but a *means of embodiment*. I often tell my students, "Where prose may *describe* a thing, poetry exists to *embody it*. If I tell you I feel sad, you'll have information about me, but you aren't likely to *feel it with me*. But if I can offer you an image, a sense memory, or a metaphor, then we can begin to share an experience." Here's a good slogan, one to write on the board: *Metaphor is a gateway to compassion*.

The First Prompt
Engage the group in a traditional game using the dice: pass out sets of red, white, and blue—at least one die of each color—and let everyone have a throw to create an opening metaphor. Have everyone write freely for ten minutes, endeavoring to create a poem based on their first results. Afterward, open the table for sharing. I strongly recommend that you—the workshop leader—participate in this first activity so you can volunteer to take the first plunge if people are reluctant to share. Doing so will usually loosen things up and boost morale. Especially if your poem is terrible.

Prelude to the Second Prompt
Chances are your group is ready for some *pure research* now, a

---

1 As well as the difference between metaphors and similes. According to a friend of mine (who may be plagiarizing someone much smarter) "similes are just metaphors that don't quite believe in themselves while metaphors are similes that believe in themselves too much."

chance to experiment with Metaphor Dice and use them in new ways. Some students may notice that they tend to get very similar results to those of their classmates. This is a good time to discuss the lyric power of repetition in poetry and the use of *anaphora, epistrophe,* and *symploce.* What happens when you deliberately repeat aspects of a poem, either the subject, action, or object?

The Second Prompt
Have each participant roll all three dice and get a metaphor. For this example, I used the paper dice, which you can fold and construct like origami cubes. The words were all chosen by my students.

My sister is an angry flute

Next, continue to roll only the white (adjectives) and blue (objects) at least four more times. Make a list of all subsequent permutations: *My sister is a pale handshake; she is a half-hearted fall, a windblown conspiracy.* Ask everyone to compose a poem in which *all of their metaphors* appear. Different versions of this prompt include, but are not limited to:

- Roll the red die once for a subject and then roll all eight white and blue dice from a complete box of Metaphor Dice, thus producing a much larger poem.
- Choose a random subject of your own—in other words, don't use any red dice—and combine it with multiple rolls of the white and blue dice.
- Have everyone in the class create their own set of dice using the paper dice and then trade their whites and blues.

The Final Prompt
It's time to collaborate! This final prompt often works best when none of the participants know one another. Start by dividing the group in half. You'll need an even number of poets. Failing that, you'll have to get in the game, too. And it *is a game.* A game of

chance.[2] This exercise will require that everyone compose eight new lines, four of them with Metaphor Dice. Participants must not show their work in progress. Everything they write must remain TOP SECRET until the game begins.

Next, select one half of the class to compose eight random questions, all starting with the word *Why*. To get you started, roll your Metaphor Dice four times and record the results as interrogative: *Why is love a broken curse? Why is my heart a reluctant meadow?* Finish your list with four questions of your own. These can be metaphoric, too, but it isn't crucial. *Why do my neighbors party all night? Why do pigeons walk that way?*

Finally, mix up the order of your eight questions so that they alternate between the ones prompted by Metaphor Dice and those that are wholly of your own creation.

At the same time, have the other half of the class perform the exact same exercise, except in the form of answers, all beginning with the word *Because*. For instance, *Because hope is a glorified party clown. Because my teacher is a handed-down bullseye.* Again, add four answers that are composed entirely by you but also begin with *Because*. For example, *Because I hate it when we run out of sugar*, or *Because I said so.* Mix these answers with the ones prompted by Metaphor Dice.

---

2 *Chance* is perhaps the greatest of angels in service of the poet. And the poet who stays faithful to chance stays new and surprising. When we're just starting to write, chances are our first good poems will be largely the result of risk-taking and happy accidents; we start writing toward a subject as if walking into a wilderness. Ideally, we acknowledge both that we don't know what we're doing and it doesn't matter. And as we go, at some point, we get into a rhythm, a groove, and end up miles off our original course, but somehow *arrived* at a new poem. Where I see many (MANY) poets get stuck is by trying to re-create their early successes by sheer will. The poem is already doomed—doomed to be almost as good as an old poem.

Now it's time to play! Have both sides pair up and face each other. When they're ready, have them trade questions and answers, rapid fire, in the sequence which they appear on their lists.

Why is love a broken curse?
Because I hate it when we run out of sugar.
Why do my neighbors party all night?
Because hope is a glorified party clown.
Why is my heart a reluctant meadow?
Because I said so.
Why do pigeons walk that way?
Because my teacher is a handed-down bullseye.

I've kept my examples playful but be prepared for some real surprises. The bigger the group, the wilder the results. And keep an eye out for moments of psychic convergence. There will almost always be combinations so acute as to seem clairvoyant. Once everyone has shared, they will very likely want to play again, switching sides. Go for it!

The Accidental Prompt

If you succeed in playing two complete rounds, this means everyone will have composed two lists each: one of questions and one of answers. But these will have been written with their attention on the game, and not on this last prompt. Ask everyone to look at their own two lists. Do the questions and answers align? Did they inadvertently write an entirely different call/response poem? I bet they did.

—*Brendan Constantine*

ABOUT THE JEDITORS

This anthology and the contest that fed into it was judged and edited by five judge/editors, informally called The Jeditors, who began every meeting with a poem to make sure that they didn't lose their enjoyment of poetry while doing the dirty work of it.

Taylor Mali, the inventor of Metaphor Dice, is an educator and spoken word poet. The author of seven books, he is a thirteenth-generation resident of New York City.

Nicole Homer is a community college educator, nerd, and author of the poetry collection *Pecking Order*. They live online at nicolehomer.com and lurk on social media as @realnicolehomer.

Jared Singer is a writer and audio engineer living in New Jersey. His first book, *Forgive Yourself These Tiny Acts of Self-Destruction,* was published with Button Poetry in 2019.

Bianca Phipps is a writer and grad student currently based in Chicago, IL. Their first chapbook, *Crown Noble,* was published with Button Poetry in 2020.

Kevin LeMaster is a Pops of five grandkids and has been married to the same woman for thirty-five years. He has several published poems and is looking for a publisher for his first chapbook.

Please Come Off-Book by Kevin Kantor

Please Come Off-Book is a tender, aching, and intimate look at the never-ending final dress rehearsal that is queerness. Written with a deft and clever hand, Kevin Kantor holds a mirror up to our nature, and damn if we don't look good!

Forgive Yourself These Tiny Acts of Self-Destruction by Jared Singer

Jared Singer's *Forgive Yourself These Tiny Acts of Self-Destruction* teaches us how to be kinder and more forgiving, and how it's always better to bend than break. As he states in a line from his fine poem "Love 1A:," *Love Is a Sandwich* for which Singer sets the table and all we have to do is eat.

Crown Noble by Bianca Phipps

Bianca Phipps' *Crown Noble* is an unapologetic glimpse into love, loss, and acceptance and how to rise above adversity with the beauty only a poet of their caliber can accomplish. Bianca shows their scars like coffee table books, dogeared and love-worn.

OTHER BOOKS BY BUTTON POETRY

If you enjoyed this book, please consider checking out some of our others, below. Readers like you allow us to keep broadcasting and publishing. Thank you!

Available at buttonpoetry.com/shop and more!

BUTTON POETRY BEST SELLERS

Neil Hilborn, *Our Numbered Days*
Hanif Abdurraqib, *The Crown Ain't Worth Much*
Sabrina Benaim, *Depression & Other Magic Tricks*
Rudy Francisco, *Helium*
Rachel Wiley, *Nothing Is Okay*
Neil Hilborn, *The Future*
Phil Kaye, *Date & Time*
Andrea Gibson, *Lord of the Butterflies*
Blythe Baird, *If My Body Could Speak*
Andrea Gibson, *You Better Be Lightning*

Available at buttonpoetry.com/shop and more!